better together*

*This book is best read together, grownup and kid.

akidsco.com

a kids
book
about

a kids book about queer mental health

by Brian Femminella

a
kids
book
about

Text and design copyright © 2023
by A Kids Book About, Inc.

Copyright is good! It ensures that work like this can exist, and more work in the future can be created.

A Kids Book About, Kids Are Ready, and the colophon 'a' are trademarks of A Kids Book About, Inc.

Printed in the United States of America.

A Kids Book About books are available online: *akidsco.com*

To share your stories, ask questions, or inquire about bulk purchases (schools, libraries, and nonprofits), please use the following email address: *hello@akidsco.com*

Print ISBN: 978-1-958825-67-9
Ebook ISBN: 978-1-958825-68-6

Designed by Jelani Memory
Edited by Emma Wolf

To my grandmother, Sharon, for showing me what unwavering love looks like. May your memory be forever held through the story of this book.

In support of glaad
who courageously fights
for the LGBTQ+ community.

Intro

How do you find your voice when society tells you to stay silent? It's difficult to watch kids who are queer struggling to live in a world that thrives on conformity. We, the queer community, are not a science experiment, a threat, or a mistake.

Finding your voice is difficult, and labels that define who dare go outside the lines of "status quo" make it nearly impossible to do so. Whether you accept queer people or not, please stop sending thoughts and prayers against hate and violence, or otherwise supporting from a distance, judging, ostracizing some kids, and forgetting that we are all human.

This book exists to help kids find their voice in a world that strives to box some kids in. You are not a threat, and who you love should always be celebrated.

I'm glad you're here.

No matter where you are on your journey, your story matters...

and so do you.

Hi, I'm Brian.

I'm from **New York**.

I'm a **skydiver**.

I'm a **soldier**.

And most importantly,

I'm queer.

I'm proud to be a part
of the LGBTQ+ community.

Being my true self has helped me recognize how important it is to defy the status quo.

But that **hasn't always been easy**.

Let's talk about a big word:

homop

hobia.

Have you ever heard that word?

Homophobia is the hate people give to queer people for who they love.

And this can happen for a lot of reasons.

People feel uncomfortable with what they don't understand.

They can be spiteful.

Or uneducated.

Or insecure.

Regardless of the reason,

homophobia is always hateful and it's always wrong.

For me, this is all too familiar.

And oftentimes, I struggled in silence.

As a kid, I was ostracized* in many ways.

*Being ostracized means to be excluded from
a group, by common consensus of the group.

I was left out.

I was attacked physically, mentally, and verbally. And people didn't believe it happened.

I was told I couldn't do certain things.

I knew people were talking about me behind my back.

I wasn't supported by the administration and teachers in my school.

I wanted a caring community, and what I got was the opposite.

I questioned my own value.

I felt...

worthless.

Mental health

wasn't something seriously discussed when I was growing up.

But all of these things took a toll on my mind, and affected my personal mental health.

When we talk about someone's mental health, **we're talking about**...

how they **feel**,

how they **respond** to
the world around them,

and how they **interpret** themselves.

But managing mental health has a whole different layer of complexity when you are in the LGBTQ+ community.

We live in a time where our differences make us targets instead of a reason to celebrate.

When hate crimes, shootings, book bans, and other acts of violence are the norm, how can anyone possibly feel safe and secure in their own community?

I signed up to be a soldier and I believe in protecting our freedoms.

Yet the people who salute me in uniform are the same ones who would disrespect me for holding another man's hand or attending a Pride event.

Although hate may seem powerful,

when we come together, anything is possible.

Hatred will always exist.

But how you choose to continue on when it seems everyone else is silencing you defines your voice.

More often than not,
we are forced to zip up

our pride.

Whether we feel afraid, or the need
to survive or protect ourselves.

We should feel free to live a life which is open and free.

To be our true selves no matter what everyone else says.

So what can this look like for you?

Wear what makes you feel like you.

Don't mask your voice because you're nervous about the pitch or the sound.

the
noise.

Do what makes you feel happy.

Be involved in the things you love, because there is space for you there.

Be uni
to yo

que

urself.

So smile, **wear bright colors**, cover your notebooks in stickers, choose the pink backpack instead of the plain one, dye your hair purple (with a grownup's help), and **remember you are who you are** and nothing else matters.

People will judge, I promise you that. And pretend they don't understand why you exist as you do.

But just being you, as wild as it sounds, is an act of...

resistance.

Resistance is...

refusing to be silenced,

fighting against the standard and living authentically,

making those who hate feel uncomfortable,

getting loud, standing up,

and never settling for anything less than equal.

Resist for every queer person who is unable to stand with us. I promise you, they are watching.

Here are a few things **I wish I knew** when I was your age:

1. Family isn't always blood. It's the people who choose you and stand with you.

2. Your queer journey is unique and yours and it's special to you.

3. Never sacrifice your happiness to please someone else's ignorance.

4. If you feel small and alone, remember you belong to a HUGE community all over the world.

You **(yes, you)** are going to make it.

I guarantee you'll be told that our differences aren't good.

But, they're amazing.

So live every day as you.

Even when it's hard.

Keep resisting. You know who you are.

Outro

Resistance is essential when things are not right. When you feel less than, it can seem like you don't matter. I can guarantee every grownup has felt this way—regardless of the circumstances.

Share your experiences. Your struggles may differ, but seeing that it is possible to persevere means everything to kids. Do not shy away from supporting those who want to defy society's expectations of normal.

This is an opportunity to show that love exists outside of one's mind and outside of the pages of this book. Kids are ready to have hard conversations, especially when so many resources are being stripped away from them. We should all want to shut down hateful rhetoric, so teach kids that the queer community is courageous, not monstrous. Love is universal—it's as easy as that.

Sincerely, every queer person

About The Author

Brian Femminella (he/him) wrote this book for any kid dealing with the fear and judgment of being in the LGBTQ+ community. For Brian, growing up in a community where being different wasn't accepted left him curious if the rest of the world treated people this way. He knew one thing for certain though: being queer in America was not always celebrated.

So, as he grew up, he chose to become a voice for those who feel powerless. He found a way to use his gift of bringing people together to build communities which support everyone. He uses writing, public speaking, and photography in an effort for social reform.

This book is meant to teach kids the importance of loving yourself, even when it seems like the world is against you. Brian's hope is that kids will learn how to navigate hate by focusing on self-love and being unapologetically themselves.

 @brianfemminella    @BrianArthurFemminella

brianfemminella.com

a
kids
book
about
~ONEY
~ Stramwasser

a
kids
book
about
BEING
INCLUSIVE
by Ashton Mota
& Rebekah Bruesehoff

a
kids
book
about
diversity
by Chernale Garden

a
kids
book
about
LEADer
SHIP
by Orion Jean

kids
bo
ab
IMM

a
kids
book
about
SAFETY
by Soraya Sutherlin, CEM
in partnership with JUDY

a
kids
book
about
CLIMATE
CHANGE
by Zanagee Artis
Olivia Greenspan

a
kids
book
about
IMAGINATION
by LEVAR BURTON

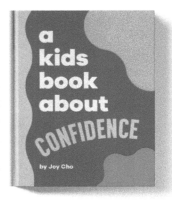
a
kids
book
about
CONFIDENCE
by Joy Cho

kids
ook
bout
XIETY
Szabo
and Happy Faces

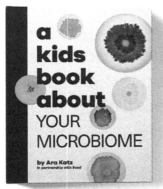
a
kids
book
about
YOUR
MICROBIOME
by Ara Katz
In partnership with Seed

a
kids
book
about
racism
by Jelani Memory

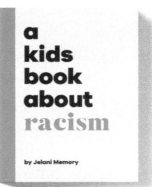
a
kids
book
about
DISABILITIES
by Kristine Napper

a
ki
b
al
ba
by KYL

a
kids
book
about
DIVORCE
by Ashley Simpo

a
kids
book
about
cancer
by Dr. Kelsie Storm & Sarah Porter

a
kids
book
about
BEING
TRANSGENDER
by Gia Parr
in partnership with The GenderCool Project

a
kids
book
about
DEPRESSION
by Kileah McIlvain

ds
ook
out

a
kids
book
about
THE TULSA

Printed in the USA
CPSIA information can be obtained
at www.ICGtesting.com
LVHW060006090124
768359LV00015B/1196